SUCCESS SECRETS FOR THE YOUNG ENTEREPRENEUR

Nate
The Great

Disclaimer

All the information, techniques, skills and concepts contained within this publication are of the nature of general comment only and are not in any way recommended as individual advice. The intent is to offer a variety of information to provide a wider range of choices now and in the future, recognising that we all have widely diverse circumstances and viewpoints. Should any reader choose to make use of the information contained herein, this is their decision, and the contributors (and their companies), authors and publishers do not assume any responsibilities whatsoever under any conditions or circumstances. It is recommended that the reader obtain their own independent advice.

FIRST EDITION 2019

Published by
Real Estate Coach Pty Ltd
1300 288 665

ISBN 9 781086 480535

"For my Family"

CONTENTS

CHAPTER 1
A YOUNG CUB

Human beings all have one thing in common, and that's the ability to grow up. I look at myself growing up, the environment that I was born in, the city, the time, the place, and I look at exactly where I'm at and where I was at that present moment. Many of us don't remember too much when we were young. We have little mini-flashbacks of whenever we were younger, but those are the moments when things were good and you didn't tend to worry as much, or you didn't tend to fear as much whenever you were a child. You didn't overthink things. Things just came naturally to you.

If somebody told you to ride a bicycle over a ramp, you would do it. You wouldn't think twice about it. It's because when you're young, you don't have much fear, you think you can take over the world, you imagine yourself just being on a couch or a reclining chair in your house but yet you feel like you're on a parachute taking over the world. You feel like whenever you're outside, and you're waving your hands up in the air, running around in circles, you feel as if you're in a helicopter, you're in an airplane flying across the world. One thing as being a kid was the imagination that we as human beings have.

We have the ability to imagine, and I remember whenever I was younger, I used to imagine being a sports athlete, I used to remember wanting to be a professional basketball player. I just wanted something to do with sports. Then as I grew older, as I went to elementary school and went to middle school, I realized the older that you get, the more robust and the harder life can get as young cubs. That's what I like to call us growing up because we start as a cub but can eventually evolve into that lion.

What do I mean by evolving? Ask yourself, what kind of environment were/are you surrounded around? How were you raised? Just these couple of things and we're going to cover more in this entire book on how to dominate YOU as a person. You'll learn how to evolve into the lion that you're meant to be. It doesn't matter where you were born, it the time, what race you are, none of that matters. What matters is that you have a gift, and you were gifted to be born in this fantastic universe.

You are the one that makes up your choices, and that determines your destiny. There might be some days, especially when growing up, where you might've got told NO, and you had to listen to your family, and that was what was realistic back then. The growing up process whenever we were really little compared to where we're at now, it's a lot different. A lot of us tend to say; I wish I could go back to being a kid, I wish I could go back to school, I wish, I wish, I wish.

Being a young child and being a young cub is truly special.

You felt that you could conquer the world; you thought that you could do anything that you wanted to in your life. If you wanted to be a doctor, a firefighter, or an athlete, you thought it was possible. You thought everything was possible. You thought to be able to travel the world was something that anyone could do, but as the older that you get when you go through middle school, and you go through high school when you meet all these different kinds of people, you realize things aren't as easy anymore. Things don't just seem like sunshine and rainbows. They aren't what they were whenever you were four or five years old; you realize life can be a little bit difficult. Life can be a little bit challenging. You start meeting new friends; you started meeting new people in school. You begin to sense that you can get a little bit competitive when it comes to sports and studying.

You start to realize that you might have a gift when it comes to a particular subject, specific sport or just as a certain talent, maybe you're a great singer or a great instrument player, or perhaps you're amazing at the piano. Perhaps you realize that you're great at just being the class leader or the class clown. Maybe you're the quiet one. Whoever you are, you know that you're different, that you have a unique trait.

But there also comes a time whenever you're hanging around your friends, whenever you're hanging around the people that you call your friends that you want to be just like them. And during school and class, you catch yourself being just like them at times, which is why you resonate so well with them. And of course, whenever you're going through school, you notice that there's a bunch of different crowds. Crowds are meaning; you have the jocks, people that are in the sports, the preps or popular group. You have people that are a part of the Geek Squad or the nerd squad. You have people that dress like they're in a rock band. You have people that are very holiday oriented. It's like their parents dress them up and it's the 4th of July every day haha.

That serves as an influence. You see all these different cultures. You meet all these different people, but at the time you don't think about it. You don't believe how different somebody like you can be from someone else. It doesn't matter what the color of someone's skin is or how they dress. But as soon as you start to grow up a little bit, you begin to have some realizations and whenever you get to middle school, and I'd say the high school phase especially, that's when you realize things can be a little bit different.

You hear about controversy, problems, fights, and you hear about arguments that people have in school with one another. You see and hear all of that, and you realize why principals are in schools. A principal in elementary school was just the leader of the school. A principal in a high school is basically like a sergeant. People look at them completely different as if he's the bad guy or the villain. Students look at teachers completely different though. But why is that? Why do people look at these authority figures in the school system differently compared to when they were younger?

It's because you had a realization of who they are and what they do. Maybe it was criticism, or your one friend said, "I can't believe they failed me! I can't believe they did this. They liked them better than me!" You have envy, jealousy, and all these things that can cross your mind. And then you have your favorite teachers that give you prizes and extra credit. You love that, and you feel as if they care way more than what the other ones do. But what people don't realize is, and what you might not realize is some people, aka some teachers, they do things the hard way because they know even though you might fail, they want you to understand that you got that grade for a reason truly. Maybe you didn't study, or you didn't care, and they don't want to give you a free handout to retry it.

And then again, you have some teachers; they'll give you a free handout. They'll give you extra credit. That's how they are as a person because that's how they were raised. Again, we all start as a cub. It all depends on the environment that you're raised in, how you're brought up, who you were brought up by, who you hung out around. Did you go to summer camp? Did you go to a particular school? What did you do when you were younger?

There's a reason why growing up that we have certain friend groups. It's because we were molded to them. I thought that being the guy that had a small friend group was the only way to get through in school. I felt that that playing video games and sports were the cool things that you could do. I didn't realize the importance of networking or establishing strong friendships with many people. I just thought that having a small friend group and a small circle was the way to do it.

I never took the time to realize just by talking to that girl or guy, how much of an impact that you can genuinely make within their lives. I look at some of the ones that I went to school with that were quiet. I didn't talk much whatsoever, and I look at the impact that I could have had that you could have. But if you're reading this and you're still in school or you know somebody that is just like this, now is your chance and now is your opportunity to make that impact. Again, it doesn't matter how you were raised; it doesn't matter the life that you thought you were meant to live. Because if you believe you are expected to live a particular life, you're wrong. You're meant to live the life that you desire.

Just because you were a cub doesn't mean that you're always going to stay cub. We can all grow into being that lion. Maybe you're at a stage in your life in school where things are tough, and your parents keep drilling you on studying, and what you need to do, that's okay it's part of the process. Control what you can control you are the one that makes up your own decisions. We are all born as young cubs, and it is up to us to go out to live the life we want and to make our own choices, to do what it is that we genuinely want to do.

CHAPTER 2
THE INTROVERTED LIFESTYLE

I believe growing up we don't have much of choice on whether we're introverted or extroverted. We adapt to our surroundings and our environment. With myself growing up, I was the one that never really talked too much. I was more so the quiet one. I believe the reason that is because my family never really put me into social settings where I had to go out and network. You'll sometimes see families; they'll do anything they can to have their child in front of the class speaking, being a leader in their class, whatever it may be. I was never the one that was in front of the class. I was never the one that was known as the leader back then as I never really wanted to take the initiative because it was never a thing in my family to take action and be the talker.

It's funny; my father is the extroverted one. He talks a lot in a significant way, and he can hold a conversation with people. My mother, on the other hand, she's more so the shy one. She's the quiet one, so I definitely took a lot of her traits but then I'm also great at being extroverted as well, which we'll talk about in this chapter more. I'm a firm believer that you're molded into whether you are introverted or extroverted in how you grow up. Again, you can't control that because the one that's in control is your family, parents, or whoever it is you've grown up with. There's a reason that you choose the friends you decide to hang around. That's based on how you're raised. Again, as I covered earlier in the earlier chapter, there's a reason that you run around with a particular group of people.

You have the jocks, the nerds, and the people that are the popular kids. You have all of those kinds of groups. There's a reason that you run around with the people that you hang out around. It's because it matches your personality. Maybe you hang around people that are of higher power or status because you want to be like them. Being introverted doesn't mean that you can't succeed. It can be a great thing, but just because you're shy doesn't mean that you're never going to open up. You're only introverted based off of what you believe. People that classify themselves as only introverts and nothing else, typically, that's how they're going to live their lives. That's why the chapter is called the introverted lifestyle. It's because they make their lifestyle. They base it off of just being introverted. Myself growing up as an introvert, I realize that I missed tons of opportunities, especially in school.

I missed out on the relationships that I could have gained with the teachers, administration, principals, and coaches. I was big into sports as soccer was the main one. I could have had much more powerful relationships with my coaches and teammates if I had opened up a little bit more. In school, I never was the best at test taking. If I only I could have opened up and said, "Hey, I need help. I'm not the best test taker. What can I do to improve this? What can you give me to improve my game and can help me?" I never opened up because I was too shy. I feared what they might say. I worried a rejection of them wanting to help me. I had all these false realities in my head because I just thought it was wasn't right to open up and to become a little extroverted. I never raised my hand in class, even if I had a question. I felt as if okay somebody would ask my question, but it never got asked, and I still lived on that day with that question.

I had to ask friends, "What do you think of this?" and they might not have even known the answer. I was scared to ask the teacher and to step up and raise my hand to ask them a question. What does this mean? What does that mean? I thought the fear of judging would come into play. I feel that's a big fear with a lot of people growing up. They fear to ask people things. They fear that they're going to get judged by everyone, but they shouldn't worry about that because you miss out on so many opportunities based off of what you think others are going to think of you. I wish I would have tried out for more sports in high school. I sometimes wonder, what would it have been like if I tried out for football? What would it have been like if I asked that girl out on a date? If I went to prom... I never went to prom. What would it have been like if I did go to prom?

I have all these different thoughts and of course us as human beings we tend to have regrets whether it's in our younger years, or they say the biggest regret for people in nursing homes is wishing they could have done more things while they were young. The people that are on their deathbeds, they wish they could have started that business. They wish they could have taken that leap of faith. I don't want to live a regret lifestyle, and I don't want you to live a regret restyle. Ask yourself, how much are you going to open up? What are you going to do to just come out of that introverted phase? I realized once I graduated high school, I didn't want to go to college or university. It wasn't as attractive to me because I knew that I just wasn't interested in school. I knew that the subjects that I was being taught just weren't something that I wanted to go out and preach in my life necessarily. I knew that I didn't want to go out and teach Calculus, Algebra, Math, Science, or History. That wasn't me. I was the motivational guy.

I was the one that wanted to impact the world by changing lives, but I still realized that I had that introverted soul in me. I realized that I had to find a way. I had to open up. I had to break the barrier of being an introvert. That's whenever I started watching a bunch of motivational videos on YouTube and found the man himself. The top motivational speaker in the world, Eric Thomas. He's the one that gave me light and helped me overcome trials and tribulations throughout my lifetime. He's the one that got me to open up and get a little more passionate. Then I got into business, and that led me to discover my gift. That's being interactive and connecting with people on a deeper level. I began to identify what my strengths were. I realized at a very young age; I'm a great listener. I've been told over and over again that I'm a great listener.

Typically, introverts are great listeners because they don't talk much, but then I realized that it's excellent to listen, but we all have a voice. Every single one of us has a light inside of us and has a voice to share with the public. Introverts have powerful voices that we can talk, and people will listen to them.

I want you to take a moment and identify your strengths. Get a piece of paper and jot down your top strengths. Maybe you're extroverted, and you're reading this. What are your top strengths? Write down those strengths. Are you a great listener? Are you a deep connector? Whenever you're in front of a classroom, speaking, how do you react? What do you feel? What are those emotions that come into play? You know yourself better than anybody else does.

Identify these critical traits within yourself. Know what you're good at, and then I want you also to jot down the things that you want to be good at. Maybe you want to be a better extrovert. Or, perhaps you want to be that leader of the class. Maybe you want to be known as the one that is the influencer or the motivator. Whatever it is that you want to do, you can do it because you are the one that makes up your decisions. Knowing your strengths is one of the biggest keys to your success, knowing what you're good at, but also having enough respect for yourself to understand what your weaknesses are. It's one thing to know what you're good at. It's another thing to know what you're not good at and what you're going to do to improve.

Here are some action steps, if you're introverted and you need to get better at public speaking. Go to Toastmasters or look up Toastmasters online and enroll in a class. I took the Dale Carnegie training when I first started. It was a nine-week training program on becoming a better public speaker. Invest in yourself. Buy some books. There's a great book called "Quiet: The Power of Introverts in a World That Can't Stop Talking" by Susan Cain. Invest in yourself because it's not going to come overnight. You got to work on it just like with dating and relationships as you're not just going to find that instant match right away. Look at yourself, because you're introverted, look at all the potential and all the opportunity that you have to maximize and to release. It's incredible, the number of things that you can do but you're the one that has to decide. You're the one that has to go to that Toastmaster event or that networking event.

Trust me; I've been there. I've done that. I've missed so many networking events because I've chickened out. I said, "You know what, I'm not feeling it today." and I made some lame excuse. "Oh, my alarm didn't go off." Yeah, it did. I just turned it off, and I said it didn't go off. Oh, I don't want to go because I'm not feeling so good today. I feel under the weather. My stomach feels a little weird. Well, guess what. That's part of the process. You're going to get butterflies. Oh, I didn't go because I scheduled a call at that time when I totally could have planned it for another time. I could have scheduled it for two hours before or two hours after, but instead, I wanted to make up in my mind and say, "Hey. I didn't go because I scheduled a call at this time." I had dinner at that time. I had a date. Whatever the excuse is, it's false. You made an excuse because you weren't confident enough to go. You felt I don't want to go to a networking or a social event because there are people there and I'm not used to that, and I get uncomfortable.

When I get uncomfortable, it makes me feel weird. It makes me nervous, and I don't like that feeling, but the thing is when you get that feeling and when you genuinely accept that feeling, that's where you grow the most. Public speaking is the number one fear in the world. Not spiders. Not death. Public speaking is the number one fear in the world. So, again, you need to identify your strengths. You need to know what your weaknesses are. If you want to crack your shell, look at yourself as a turtle. A turtle can close themselves into that shell, and they're an introvert, but when they come out of that shell, they put their arms, legs, and stick that little head out of the shell so you can see them. They're in extroverted mode — same thing with the cub and lion analogy. A lot of us were/are cubs. We're brought up as cubs, but for you to become that lion, you need to take note on what it is that you're going to do to make that change.

Naturally, I'm introverted at heart, but I know being a businessman and with what I do that having an extroverted side helps a ton. It's amazing what you can do. Being introverted, we're great listeners. We can listen all day to someone and what they have to say. Typically, introverted people, when they listen to others, it drains their energy, but extroverted people can talk forever. Extroverts speak a lot as that's what drains their energy after a while. Your listening skills might be the most excellent suit in your personality, but how can you use your listening skills to become more extroverted? Maybe you're the type where you listen a lot, but you can interrupt from time to time-based off of the conversation. Perhaps you're so great at listening that you let the person talk for an hour. Instead of letting them speak for an hour, you made them aware you want to chime in.

You could say, "Hey listen, is it cool if I interrupt? Do you mind if I cut you off one second and just let you know my feedback?" Don't be scared to speak up. Just because you're introverted, that doesn't mean that you can't speak up. You decide what it is that you want to say and what you want to do. Your listening skills are super important, but you have to know when to activate speaking up and when to interrupt. Politely, of course. Something else as introverts and the introverted lifestyle is having your alone time. If you're an introvert, alone time is so crucial. Every single day I need my alone time because I know myself. I know who I am as a person and I know if I don't have enough alone time, I can get irritable. My personality is meant to have some time for myself. We're all meant to have alone time because that's the time where you get to self-reflect. Whether it's for the day, the year, the month, or week. Maybe you got off an important phone call. Have some alone time to think about it.

Even if it's for five minutes a day, don't make an excuse saying you're so busy you don't have enough time for it. It doesn't matter who you are. It doesn't matter if you know you're Arnold Schwarzenegger, the President of the United States, or the busiest man in the world. You can still make time to have that alone time. To be yourself. You might have kids. The kids can be screaming, they can be loud but take some time out every single day because that's where you get to plug in and recharge yourself. It's a fantastic feeling. It's great going out and networking. It's great doing all these social events and meeting new people, but at the end of the day, there's no better feeling than just being in a room with you.

Even extroverts need their alone time but for the introverts, the alone time might already be there. If the alone time is already there, now you need to have a balance.

You're so great at the alone time, but that might be keeping you balled up inside for being extroverted. The solution to this is you need to go out more. Maybe you need to make a goal, and you don't need to shock yourself from the start. If you like to go all in perhaps, you do need to shock yourself, but if you want to ease your way into it gradually, I challenge you to go to one social or one networking event every single month. The funny part is you don't even have to talk. You can go for the experience. You can get around that energy, and it's going to make you feel uncomfortable. You're going to want to talk being around a lot of people as the energy grows on you. Just the fact that you go to a networking or a social event, a conference and you put yourself out there it goes to show that you have the courage. You have what it is that people are looking for, and people are looking to interact with you. You might have somebody come up and you and say, "Hi. What's your name?" You say your name, and the conversation starts.

A lot of people think networking is hard and that being an introvert means you can't open up. That's bogus. We tend to complicate our circumstances a lot more. We tend to say they're a lot more complicated than what they are, but they're not. We're in our head way too much. I can't do this because I'm quiet. I can't be a public speaker because I was never raised to be extroverted. If we're talking about real life, I can't be a millionaire because I was never born into a millionaire family. I started from the bottom, so I'm never going to make it to the top. If you live by that, you're living in a big, fat lie. I could name all day the success stories of people going from the bottom to the top. You don't have to be born with a silver spoon in your mouth. I would instead not be born with a silver spoon in my mouth because I want to experience every single inch and every single bit that it takes actually to achieve success and not just to be given victory from the start.

There's a difference, and because you're in your head too much, that is what gives you the false reality of you saying that you can't do it because you weren't granted or you weren't gifted. Ladies and gentlemen, we're all gifted. We all have a gift, and that's the gift of life. Now we all have individual gifts as well. Some of us are great listeners, great talkers, great at sports, and excellent at business. Don't get in your head too much because that's when you start over thinking. Go with your intuition. If you know that you need to go out and network, DO IT. Don't say, "Well, what if I go out, and I meet somebody that I don't want to meet." So what! That's life. Do your thing. Go out. Meet new people. Get uncomfortable. Who cares how you look. I don't know what to wear. So what!

Just wear something. Wear a t-shirt. Stand out because I guarantee you when you go out in public, people are thinking the same thing about themselves. I wonder if I look okay? I wonder what I look like? I wonder what I feel like?

We're all human beings that operate the same way. We're not perfect but people that have already achieved success, they're just more confident. They know what it takes because they've already been there. What you're going through is exactly what they've gone through. Nobody's born with confidence. Nobody's born with just instant success to keep it. Now some people, don't get me wrong; they are born with some incredible genes. They have beautiful looks but remember you can control how much you think in your head. That is entirely up to you. Communication is another big thing; being introverted and learning how to communicate correctly. Having that balance can be one of the most challenging jobs there is by just going out and interacting with people. There's a thing that they call a five-foot rule. If there's somebody five feet in front of you, make an attempt. Ask them, "Hey, how's your day?" Compliment them.

I fly a good bit and travel a lot. Whenever you're checking your bags, ask the baggage check woman or gentleman how their day is going. Smile at them because they talk to so many people. If you're in a drive through getting food or you're out in public, and you know the person that's been working the cash register, they've probably checked out hundreds of people that day, be that light. Be that one that shines and brightens their entire day up. Don't just be that one that goes through the line and you don't talk to them whatsoever. Talk to them. Show them who you are. Show them that they're there. Show them that they're alive, that they're present just because you're the one going through the line. Communicate with them. How was your day? Do you give anything fun planned for the holidays? Be cool about it. Be genuine. Be real and don't fake it. Okay, people can feel that. People can sense when others tend to fake it.

Communicate with your family. Maybe there's a gap in your family where you haven't communicated well with them. Communication is one of the biggest things in life, especially when it comes to partnerships and relationships. If a couple, business partnership, or friendship doesn't know how to communicate properly, I hate to say it, but it's probably not going to work out. That's why divorce rates are so high is because of a lack of communication. You need to understand people's needs. If you're in a relationship, you need to understand your partner's needs. When was the last time that you asked them how they felt about your current situation within your marriage or relationship? Maybe this is something you need to address. When was the last time that you had a genuine conversation over the phone with a loved one? When was the last time that you told somebody that you loved them, that you admire them, that you're grateful for them?

This is the communication that you need to evaluate for yourself and see where you're at with it. Communication is one of the most critical and absolute greatest attributes we can use to our advantage, but being an introvert has led us not to communicate as much, which leaves people in the dark. They don't know what you're thinking in your head. We're not mind readers. We're as great as each other. Whenever you're not talking or whenever you're just sitting there quiet, people think what is that person thinking? Express yourself. It's okay to think but express yourself. Be more talkative. Communicate with people. Typically, introverts don't do so well in group settings. It's because it's overwhelming. I'm not the best at group settings but I know that's a weakness and I know that's what I need to work on. So, again, identify what you're good and what you're not so good at. Identify how good you are at communicating and what you need to work on with communication.

If you're not the type that wants to go out to events, I challenge you to record a video of yourself talking. I know it might be a little bit uncomfortable, but I challenge you to record a video of you. If you want a more significant challenge, I challenge you to send it to your friend and get their feedback on what they think of you. Whatever they think of you, it doesn't matter because you're the one that decided to make the video in the first place. Something else I like to go into is you sometimes need to pretend to be an extrovert. Now, I do business, and I talk with a lot of people, and not everybody is introverted, so I need to be extroverted. So I play to their strengths. I realize that with them being extroverted, I got to be somewhat not exactly like them, but I have to match them in a way. I need to become more extroverted, so there's not an awkwardness to the conversation because you'll meet people that are extroverted that can talk all day and you can be quiet and not speak at all, and they'll love that.

It's kind of like that 70/30 rule. Have that person talk 70% of the time, and you talk 30% of the time but don't make it where they speak 90%, and you talk 10%. Either way, they're going to walk away feeling like wow I enjoyed that conversation because they spoke the entire time, but you want to make it somewhat semi-balanced which is a 70/30. 70/30 is what you want because you want to ask them the questions and you want to be extroverted. Again, don't be afraid to interrupt them. Ask them questions. Have enthusiasm when speaking. Don't be scared to go on a little bit of a rant because you're the one that's pretending to be extroverted. Guys, I'm not extroverted. I'm introverted, but I'm great at pretending to be extroverted because I realize we can be whatever we say we want to be. Now, I'm not a basketball player. I'm not the next Shaquille O'Neal. That's a gene thing, but when it comes to communication and pretending to be something, we can do that.

That's called manifestation. We're visualizing what we're good at. Visualize that you're an extrovert. If you go to a social setting, imagine that you're the most talkative person in that room. I guarantee you'll build confidence. Now, let's talk a little bit more about extroversion. There are perks about being an extrovert. Being an extrovert means, you're typically the one that's going to be talking in front of people. You're always the outgoing one. You don't have a hard time holding a conversation. You're always the go-to guy who typically most people want to be. It's because they're so used to hearing your voice. You're usually the one in the workplace that is the leader. You're typically the one that's on the sports team who is the captain. You might be the class clown even. So there are lots of things when being an extrovert that it's great to be. There's a lot of perks at being great at extroversion.

Extroverted people tend to hold conversations longer, which means that whoever they're speaking with they can talk in more extended time frames, which is crucial because introverts can't always do that. Extroverts, they're great at doing that. Extroverts are great at just holding conversations as they're outgoing and they don't have a hard time just talking to anybody. They can pretty much strike up a conversation with anybody which if we're talking in life and in business that's a great thing because you never know who you're going to meet. Typically, introverts are the opposite, and they mess up on opportunities. Extroverts tend to also gain more opportunities just by talking. It's a beautiful thing. Something else that introverts need to realize is the power of speaking — the power of their VOICE.

If you're introverted, people realize that you don't speak as much. So whenever you do talk and whenever you do get up and give a speech, or you are called upon, and you do decide to speak up, people are going to focus on you because they don't get a chance to hear from you much in the first place. Which is what makes you rare, it's what makes you unique, so you need to live up to that. If you're introverted, live up to the times when you get a chance to speak because you might not get to talk much and people realize that but when you do speak, you capture everybody's attention in the room. Personally, myself, I've been able to do this plenty of times, and people listen to you because one thing about being an extrovert, people are so used to hearing from you. People are so used to hearing you talk but when an introvert talks and they're not used to talking, or people aren't used to that, they want to listen, and it captures their attention instantly because introverts don't open up like that.

Introverts aren't the ones to speak and to go on a rant and to give a public speech and to offer advice and feedback, but when they do, their voice is so powerful because people want to hear from them. People want to hear from you, and that's why you need to speak up more. That's why you need to challenge yourself to ask questions. Don't be afraid to go out and ask somebody something. Don't be scared to give out that compliment; your voice is so powerful. Just because you're introverted doesn't mean that you can't go out and make a name for yourself. There's plenty of successful introverts. Steve Wozniak, one of the founders of Apple, Bill Gates, Albert Einstein, Edgar Allan Poe, these guys, were all introverts and look at the success that they've had. So when you look at some of the greatest of all time and with what they've achieved and knowing that they're introverts and with what they've accomplished, it's an incredible feeling.

You don't just have to be an extrovert to see success. You can be an introvert and have success. The list goes on. You can go on Google and type up successful introverted people, and you'll have a whole list of people that pop up. Even presidents are introverted. Some presidents are shyer than others. Some are extroverted. The introverted people that are successful, it's funny, the statistics are a bit higher in terms of income made because typically introverts think a lot more than what extroverts do which means they can strategize their plans. They have more thinking time. So usually and I read this in a book, introverts are more likely to have more so of a higher net worth than extroverts which if you are an introvert, it's great to hear that. It builds more confidence within you because, again, we tend to think more about things which are good, but if you know how to balance it at the end of the day, that will win things over for you a lot more.

So, again, ladies and gentlemen, just because you're introverted doesn't mean that you can't make a name for yourself. You can go out and do whatever it is that you want to do. You live the life that you want to live. If you're going to be extroverted, be an extrovert. If you're going to stay introverted, stay an introvert. Whatever it is that your goal is, you can go out and achieve. You create your lifestyle. I labeled this chapter, The Introverted Lifestyle because I wanted to let you know precisely the lifestyle that most people live in. The false reality that people have of themselves. Something else that you can do for some action steps is to take a personality test. Know who you are. There's plenty of quizzes online. I recommend taking one; it's called the Myers-Briggs Personality Test. There are sixteen personality types. It's a great test to take as it gives you four letters that you are personality wise. If you're introverted or extroverted, if you're intuitive or you're feeling, if you're judging, or you're sensitive.

Identify yourself. I recommend going on Google, searching up the Myers-Briggs Personality Test. That's a huge one. Another one is the '4 Animals Assessment' otherwise known as the DISC Assessment. It's a personality test, but you get to discover on a deeper level more so than the personality test what animal you are. Look up on Google the '4 Animals Assessment'. You can either be a gorilla, flamingo, turtle, or a chameleon. Which one are you? There's only one way to find out, and that's by taking a test, and that will help you identify who you are as a person and that will determine what your personality type is, what you're good at, and what you can improve on. I recommend self-education and personal development. As an introvert, we tend to do more things like this because we want to identify who we are as a person. Once you truly know who you are, then you can adjust and adapt to who you want to become.

The introverted lifestyle, it's not easy. But we can control the lifestyle that we want, and it's entirely up to you to make that change. So, I challenge you to write down a list of as many things as you can that you're good at. Is it listening? Maybe you're great at test taking. What is it that you're good at? What are some things that you can improve upon? This isn't just for being introverted. This is also if you're extroverted. Then what I want you to do is, I want you to circle the ones that stand out, the ones that you're great at, and the ones that you need to improve on. I want you to do whatever it takes to become better at those. So, maybe you got to buy some books on how to become a better listener. Perhaps you got to buy some books on how to become more extroverted. I want you to challenge yourself to find all the possible solutions to figure out how to strengthen your weaknesses because there's power behind that.

I want you to take a personality test. I want you to take the '4 Animals Assessment'. Read more books. Challenge yourself, but I want you to challenge yourself to identify who you are as a person. That's the whole purpose of this chapter. Identify who you are. Know who you are. Accept who you are. Don't just change who you are because you are you for a reason, but what you can change is what you can become better at. Maybe you're in school, perhaps you're a businessman, a businesswoman, or you have a corporate job, and you want to get promoted. Focus on these things based off of these tests and what you already know you're good at and what you need to improve on. Focus on the things that you need to improve on and get good at and then apply that into your everyday life whether it's relationships, whether it's with work, whether it's just going out in public. Improve on these things. Practice and, sure enough, you'll see the results start to flood in. You'll achieve amazing things. You'll achieve incredible and remarkable results. Take action now.

CHAPTER 3
CHOOSE YOUR CIRCLE WISELY

I'm a firm believer that this circle that you have, meaning the people that you surround yourself with has a tremendous impact on your life. Myself growing up, I never really did a lot of networking. So, I had a tiny circle, and I remember I kept a lot to myself. When I got into high school, and in middle school, I started to realize who are some of my friends. I realized that there was like a lower class, a middle class, and a higher class in school.

I feel like the lower class was those that didn't necessarily talk too much, and they were kind of like the people that were so different. You had the rock group kind of people, the people that were just labeled differently. Then you had the middle class, which are the people that talked a little bit. They tried to talk to people that were lower and the higher class, but they wanted to more so be in their own lane. They had their own little group, and they were associated with that. They didn't care if they were well known. They just wanted to be themselves. I was part of the middle group. And then, there was a higher group, which were the people that more wanted the attention, they were pretty much the front of the class. They were the leaders. They were the people that played sports mostly.

I was in the middle class, the group that stuck together. We had our own little groups in school we gathered around the lunch table. You talked about the game yesterday, the soccer game we played the weekend before. We talked about the next video game that was coming out. How much we were going to play that game together. And, that was my circle growing up.

I was the person that was the gamer. I wanted to be the best of the best when it came to video games and winning every single game, the same as sports. That's how I was. I was competitive, and I always wanted to strive to do my best, while also having fun with those that were around me. I had lots of fun. I had a great time. Sometimes, which was rare, I used to get in trouble, but from time to time, whenever you're having fun with people that you enjoyed spending time with, things like that tend to happen.

I noticed that once high school came to an end, I slowly started to weed people out of my life. Because I realized, and I'd say more so towards the senior year, and mid-senior year, and towards the end of senior year, I realized that I was having kind of a mental shift. And, that mental shift was, wow, these people, really, they're cool, they're great to be around, but are they helping me grow? Are they the group that's going to help me thrive, to get to the next level? And, at the time, I was getting into motivational videos and inspirational videos, of course, with Eric Thomas being a significant influence. Watching his motivational videos helped me so much, and with the principles and lessons that he was speaking, they didn't quite align to the traits that I had, to what I was living by every single day.

I noticed that, and with me taking that into perspective, I realized that it was time to cut some people out. I didn't have a hard time doing that. Once we graduated high school, I pretty much said, it's all me. It's my time. It's nothing else. I knew that playing video games; I wasn't going to make a living off of that. I knew that I had to give up these little small things, I sold my game systems, I sold these little things that didn't quite bring value to me, and that didn't quite fulfill me adequately. The idea is they fulfill you temporarily. They don't satisfy you to your fullest. And, that's something I was fortunate enough to identify early on. I wish I could have recognized that earlier on when I was in school.

You need to think about distractions. Is your inner circle right now, distracting you? Maybe some of you have an inner circle with a few people in it. There might be 10, 20 people in others circle which is cool but the smaller, the better especially with the core group. Try to stick with five people.

So, with that in mind, are they distracting you? Are they asking you, hey, let's go out on the weekend and party it up. Let's go waste time by just walking the streets, doing absolutely nothing at all. Let's go on social media and scroll, scroll, scroll, scroll, scroll. Oh, did you see what's her face yesterday? Are they the type that gossips? Are they the type that always tries to bring the negative out of people? What are they doing to benefit you? Are they benefiting you whatsoever? Are they helping you with your goals? Are they helping you stay on track of what it is that you're trying to accomplish in your life? And, if that's not the case, if they're not helping you knock out goal after goal, or at least holding you accountable, saying, hey, Nate, did you accomplish this goal by the date that you said you're going to? If not, why? Do you have people like that in your life that are merely striving to make you better? If your group isn't striving to make you better, I mean, I'm sorry to say, but you're going to have to cut people out.

That's just the name of the game. So, you have to eliminate all distractions, AKA people that don't push you. Just because you have fun hanging out with John down the street, it doesn't always mean that he's going to help benefit you in your life. Now, I'm not saying just because you've had a long childhood friend ever since the beginning of school, which was in elementary school, I'm not saying you have to cut them out. Trust me; I still have one or two childhood friends that I had back in elementary school to this day because we have that bond, and we have that connection. But I know when I need to lay my foot down, and I know when business needs to get done, compared to when the playtime needs to be. I have that balance. Some of you guys, you don't have that balance.

They're distractions in your life, and the friends that are the distractions are those that are always wanting to take from you. They always ask you to do this, to do that. What are the distractions? Who are the distractions in your life? And, once you figure that out, that's when things start to change. Write it out on a piece of paper, write out your distractions, and then once you take note of who they are, then that's when everything starts to shift. That's when you begin to identify, wow, I was in a mental fog.

Now, what I want you to focus on is the influence. Who is influencing you and your life? Is it your family? Is it some of your friends? Maybe you got influenced by somebody that you had no idea who they were. Perhaps they held the door open for you, or maybe you saw a couple walking down the street, and you saw the boyfriend open the car door for his girlfriend. What is the influence within your life, meaning your circle? Who is it that influences you and your circle? Maybe you're the influence in your sphere. But you need to get to the point where, instead of you being the influence, you have other people that are of significance in your circle. Because if you're the only influence in your circle, yes, people are always going to look up to you, but you still need somebody to look up to, AKA a mentor, because having a mentor can help grow you immensely.

It'll grow your circle of tenfold, more than you can ever imagine. It's an incredible feeling. I'm not saying that you have to have a hundred mentors. I'm saying get people that can influence you as a person. Because if you're in a circle right now that you don't have any influence, then you need to think back, and you need to think hard on, how can I change this? How can I change my current circumstances? How can I separate myself to become an influence? Who can I go to that can help me become an influence? I need you to think about that. Are you getting influenced? And if not, why? Ask yourself that question. Why are you not getting influenced? Why is your circle, not the influence that you want it to be? These are things that you need to ask yourself, and you need to have a real conversation because by not having a circle of influence, it doesn't help. You need people that are going to strive and push you to the next level. Influence is key.

It is draining or inspiring. Are people draining you, or are people inspiring you? Do you have people that are always, like I said, taking, taking, taking, taking, taking from you every single day? They want to know every single thing about you. They want to see what you're doing and how you're doing it. Are these people constantly draining you? Look at yourself as a battery. I look at some of these rechargeable batteries. Everything needs to be recharged. Even a car battery needs a recharge. After so long it sits, so it's draining every single day. But how's it going to get more power. By running it. That's the point of having a vehicle.

We're the same way. We get drained by being around the wrong people. And again, it's your circle that you surround yourself with. So, are the people that you're around 24/7, maybe it's your work environment, college, school, or family environment. The family environment can be very draining. And, the reason I say this is because a lot of people, they like to gossip. Whether they're in your family or just in your circle that wants to gossip and talk about other people, that's going to be draining to you.

That's just going to spread negativity. Depending on what your goals are in life if you're wanting to get to the next level, having that negativity and draining people in your life, it's not going to help you whatsoever. So, you need to get to ask yourself where can I find people that are inspiring? Maybe you've got to move out. You have to get to the point on what it is that you want. Perhaps you already know the type of person that you want to be inspired by. Maybe you don't. Take out a piece of paper and write down who the ideal person that I want in my life to inspire me is? What are those traits?

Once you know that answer to that question, then you can go out and find that person. But, for you to find that person, you've got to be willing to go out and make the efforts. This person isn't just going to show up on your doorstep one day and knock on your door and say, hey, I'm that inspiring person that you've been looking for. Sometimes you have to search. Again, this is where your personality type comes into play. Like we talked about in the previous chapter. You know what makes you click.

There's somebody out there in the world that is inspiring, that's just like you, that you're going to look up to. But, you're the one that needs to find them. You need to be the one that's going to cut these people out that are draining you. You need to find the ones that are going to inspire you to be great, encourage you to be better, and inspire you to keep going. Trust me, you're going to have moments in your life where you feel down, you feel like you're defeated, and you need those people to lift you up. You need that support system. You need that group. That's going to be huge to your success. Choose your circle wisely.

If I were starting from scratch again and was listening to this or reading this, and I was thinking, okay, I need somebody. I need a group of people for my circle. I would pick people that are totally above my level because I want to learn consistently from these people every single day, every single hour, every single minute. I want to learn from these people continually. Because I know I'm challenging myself. And, that's something that you need to do. You need to challenge yourself to find these kinds of people. Go on social media, send people DM's, send people messages, send people emails saying that you're looking for somebody for help. Invest in yourself. Invest in some programs. I've invested in myself ever since I was 15 years old. I bought my first personal development book. I've gotten into programs that have accountability partners that have systems like this because I realized how important it was early on to get into an arrangement with hungry people, or others that are rooting for you to succeed and help get you to the next level.

Age is just a number, and it simply doesn't matter. It doesn't matter if you're 12 years old. It doesn't matter if you're 90 years old. It doesn't matter what age you are; you need to challenge yourself to find these groups of people. Don't be scared. Don't be shy. Don't say, oh, I'm in too small of a town. I'm in too small of a city. That's an absolute false reality. The reality is you don't want to find that person because you don't feel comfortable going out and making that effort. You need to get to a point where you're comfortable by going out, meeting new people, and going to networking events.

Are you challenging yourself to find these types of people? I'm going to be honest with you; if you're looking for greatness, if you're looking for people that are going to inspire you, they're not just going to come to your house. They're not just going to hit you up. They're not just going to be on the streets randomly. You're going to have to go to events. You're going to have to go to a networking event, a networking party, or a social event, maybe you have to enroll again into an online university. Perhaps you have to join a community and pay 50 bucks a month, or 20 dollars a month, whatever it is. You have to take the challenge, and you have to accept the challenge because if you want your life to grow substantially and your network AKA your circle of influence to drastically improve, then you need to make the change and you need to challenge yourself to grow. Because if you're not going to grow, your circle is not going to grow. And, you're just draining yourself every single day. Challenge yourself.

And, I want to end this chapter by saying, I challenge you to go onto social media and connect with somebody. Connect with somebody that might be a higher power that has more of influence or is very influential. I recommend somebody that isn't too influential. For example, if somebody goes after Tony Robbins. I'm not saying you're not going to be able to get connected with him, but you're going to want to invest, if you go after somebody like him, I would invest into some of his courses. I want you to look at somebody that might be just the same age as you and they're doing something remarkable, they're doing something great, but you still can have access to them, just by sending them a DM, and they're more likely going to reply just by sending them a message.

So, I want you to reach out to somebody that is of high influence, and I want you to invest in some of the courses they offer. Maybe they have a book, course, or a community you can invest in. Then, the second challenge is I want you to message somebody random. Reach out to someone that isn't too far ahead of you, but they're still doing well for themselves. Make sure they seem accessible. Send them a DM. Chances are they might not respond. Follow up and send them another message. Engage with them. Even call them if you have too.

They might say, hey, I'll charge you a small fee of $50 a month to coach you. Accept it. Maybe if you get lucky, they'll do it for free. Challenge yourself to make these steps. Challenge yourself to grow. Because if you want your circle to grow, you need to grow. And, if you're going to get rid of all these distractions and draining people, you're the one that is going to need to change. So, it all comes back to you; you're the one that needs to challenge yourself. So go challenge yourself. Do it NOW.

CHAPTER 4
OUTLIER MENTALITY

When you hear the word outlier, what comes to mind? When I first heard the phrase outlier, I was a bit lost. I didn't quite understand what the word meant. I always thought something mathematical... I didn't do too good at math!

But to me, an outlier is somebody that stands out from the group. Somebody willing to do whatever it takes and knows what they're good at, and is gifted. Someone that is going all in 24/7. They want success. They'll do whatever it takes. That's what makes them an outlier.

Growing up, I didn't quite identify myself as an outlier. In high school, when I realized the group I was hanging around; they just weren't the ideal friend group. They just weren't the right circle as I talked about previously in the last chapter.

I realized that I was a little bit different. I realized that the way that I began to think, the way that I operated daily was utterly different. I had a gift, and I was special.

I started to watch motivational videos and read books about success. Which, where I'm from that is strange and odd to do. That's not a thing because I'm from a very conservative town where we've never really had a successful celebrity like person besides a handful that you can count on one hand to be successful. That was just never a thing.

Whenever I started to read books about success, I used to get looks in my class. I used to have people come up to me and say, "Why are you watching that Nate? What's wrong with you? What is this book about? This book looks terrible. It just doesn't look right. Why are you reading about success? Do you think you're going to be successful? What is this guy teaching you here on this screen? What has he been through?"

I had all of these negative minds try to come into my life because people saw what I was doing, and they saw that I was trying to level up. But where I'm from that's not necessarily the thing to do in terms of leveling up. People always want to bring you down from back home here.

I'm not saying that's everybody, but a majority of the people that I had a class with they questioned me. Even my close friends, I realized that I was different because they never were into the same things.

And they even started to turn on me saying, the stuff that I was listening to, they're doing it to take my money. They don't mean what they say. They're just doing it to scam me. And I thought that was a big fat lie just getting told to me.

And that was another reason that I decided to go out on my own, and do my own thing, and cut a lot of people out because I realized from early on that I was different. And from whenever I graduated high school and went to my first ever personal development conference, I realized that this was a life that I wanted. This was the life that I wanted to live.

And that was striving for greatness, always leveling up and being around the right people, being around people that motivated you as I realized that I was different from everybody else — especially being young for my age back in school.

The thing about being young, a millennial, and still being in the teenage years when I was, I was open to so many things. And I think that's one of the greatest things that you can genuinely discover in yourself growing up is being open and hearing out all the different possibilities of a career — all of the various options of the life path that you want to go with.

I genuinely believe that I was chosen to be the outlier of my hometown. I truly believe that I was meant to be the one that separates himself from all the other people that said that they couldn't do it, or they can't do it because they're from a town that is not huge like a city. It's not a town where you can make a name for yourself. I'm from a town where there's nothing but warehouses and farm fields around here.

So I realized that I was very different just by the habits that I had, reading books, watching videos. I started to play fewer video games because I realized that they just weren't important to me.

I started to use social media to post motivational quotes and motivational messages. And I got messages saying, "Why are you posting this? This just isn't you." I've had people that have said, "This just isn't the Nate that I know." And I decided that I was going to stay the outlier. That was me.

I shifted my mindset and committed. I said, "You know? I'm not going to settle being normal. I'm not going to be average because I am never going settle for less than mediocre and less than average. I always want to keep striving for greatness."

And I did. I didn't necessarily strive for greatness in school because I realized that just wasn't what I wanted. And I realized towards the end of things that I wanted more than just an education.

That's why I didn't go to college because I felt that getting a degree just wasn't in my value system. At least not right now. And at least not then. It just wasn't me. That's whenever I realized that I was meant to do something within the customer service realm of things, within the people industry.

I soon discovered that business was what I was meant to do. I realized that having a job just wasn't something that I could hold because I always wanted to live on my terms. I always wanted to make the choices based off of how I preferred. I had that entrepreneurial mentality ever since I was young.

I realized that my first job, I never could grasp the feeling of listening to somebody else's commands in such a small corporate environment. That just wasn't me.

I realized that punching in and out every single day and being late, or asking to take a break or asking to use the bathroom. I realized that it was foolish and I shouldn't have to do that. I should be able to make that decision on my terms.

I thought just school was the only place that I was going to realize being an outlier was different. But I even identified early on having job after job; people didn't get me. They didn't understand who I was. They didn't get the questions that I asked.

I remember in the interviews I used to ask questions, and they used to be shocked by the responses, and the questions that I asked them. I was asking them, "Why do you want to hire me?" Instead of, why do they want to hire me? Of course, I could always answer those questions with fulfillment because the why always made sense to me.

But to them, it just didn't add up. I could see that with me being the outlier, and me understanding people at a young age, they realized that I knew something that they didn't. And that I could see right through them within an instant with the questions that I asked, and just by the way that I observed them.

They knew I was different. And I even got to the point in my job where people tried to take me down and criticize me because they knew I was different. And I could slowly and surely feel the envy and the jealousy that started to form.

You're going go through that. Being an outlier isn't easy. Nobody said it was easy. Is it worth it? Absolutely. It's a process. You have to identify what you're great at. You have to know what your traits are.

I identified that my most important traits are again; I'm a great listener, and I'm very self-aware of who I am. And with that in mind, I'm very in tune with other people. I was willing to take the extra steps to make sure the job got done, even over my bosses, managers, and their bosses.

I knew what my potential was, and they saw it as well. They were in their 40s, 50s, and saw that they knew what I could do. They wished they could have had the same opportunities that I had. I get messages every single day about this. "Nate, I want to start. I want to be like you. How did you do it?" Every single day.

And it comes back to being an outlier. What are you going to do whether it's in your town, in your city, or wherever you're from? What are you going to do to separate yourself from everybody else truly? What are you going do to truly show up in your industry, in your profession, and your work area?

I'm not saying the whole corporate structure and the entire job thing that that's not for you. Maybe that is for you. It wasn't for me. If it is for you, what are you going to do to separate yourself to be one of the highest employees that makes a name for himself in your company or their company?

These are questions you need to ask yourself because again, if you're not willing to honestly think about this, and have the real conversation, it's going to be very difficult for you to become an outlier.

There are times where you're going to think; you're strange and even weird. Good. It's great to be weird. It's great to be different. I look at myself in the mirror every single day, and I know that I'm different. I know that I'm a little bit insane and that I have a touch of insanity in me. But that's what makes you an outlier.

Thomas Edison was an outlier. Benjamin Franklin was an outlier. The great Napoleon Hill, Winston Churchill, all of these guys were outliers. Martin Luther King was an outlier. What do all these people have in common?

They all have some inspiration. They all have a motivation. They all have a why. They all know what it is that they want. They all live for a mission. And their mission is to inspire and make the world a better place to empower. That's what makes then an outlier.

Let's shift it a little bit. Let's change the state of mind. Let's move your perspective. What is it inside you that you want to do? What do you want to do? Do you want to change the world? Great.

How are you going to change the world and make it a better place? How are you going to shift your mentality if you're from a small town and you think small, who are you going to become and will you think big? Who are you going to cut out? What are you going to become?

What is the best version that you want to become? Who is it that you look up to? Don't copy them. But how is it that you want to mirror them, their principles, and their values? What is it, and how are you going to realize that you're different? And that you are going to be the outlier that you're meant to be. What are your unique traits?

Are you a great listener, talkative, or comforting? Are you looked at as an authority or a leader? What are you? We can be any single trait there is as we're human beings. We're actors. That's why there are movies because people act.

We can fake it until we make it. But honestly in your heart, what is it that you're good at? I can't answer that for you as you're the only one that can answer that. I might see something in you. But you truly know what's in you.

Responsibilities for being an outlier is not easy. They're people that identify themselves as an outlier, but whenever they see the responsibilities that they have to take on, they're not willing to do it.

It's kind of like that saying, "The richest place on Earth is a graveyard." That's because people had talents, but they didn't execute on those talents. They shied away and got scared because they realized all the responsibilities and all the duties that came with being an outlier.

Being an outlier isn't easy. It's one of the most challenging things you can ever do on the face of this earth. Because there's challenges, trials, and tribulations that you're going to go through like no other.

You're going to have to do things that don't want to do. You'll have to get up on stage to give that speech. You'll have to get up in front of hundreds of people, depending on what it is that you're doing.

You'll have to do all of these different things. By being an outlier, you're going to have to be in front of people.

You look at somebody like Steve Jobs and what he did with Apple. He was still in front of people: Edgar Allen Poe, the famous poet. Still in front of people. Yes, he had alone time. He had that balance, but he's known for his poems.

Leonardo Da Vinci, the famous painter, was still in front of people. He was well known. If you want to make a name for yourself, you have to be willing to make an effort to go all in and to become well known.

There's a reason people know who Mark Zuckerberg, Bill Gates, Steve Jobs, and who Richard Branson is. Because they decided to take control of their lives, they realized the responsibilities, and they seized those responsibilities.

Was it easy? Of course not. But you never hear about the guy that could have invented the next Facebook. You never hear about the guy that finished in second place, but you always hear about Usain Bolt because he finishes in first. You never hear about the guy that finishes in second EVER.

Same with Michael Phelps. It's always the guy that finishes first. It's still the team that finishes first. It's always the person, the individual that finishes first because nobody truly cares about the others who finish in another place. And I'm being real. Nobody cares about the person/team that finishes second.

People want the headline. What's your headline? With great headlines comes responsibility. If you're going to make an excellent name for yourself, you'll have to take control. You'll have to take responsibility. And it's not easy. Don't get in your head.

Once you start to see success, do not get into your head saying, you don't think you can do this. Or, if you're given an opportunity, seize the opportunity. Don't get in your head saying, "What if I do this?" Don't say what if.

Go all in. Say, "I AM speaking in front of thousands of people!" Never say, what if, because if you say what if, you doubt yourself. And the second that you begin to doubt yourself, things can turn South for you.

You need to know who you are before you even know who you are. Okay, I'll repeat it. Know who you are before you truly know who you are. Because when you know who you are, you act like that person. You act as if you're already that person.

If you know that you're already a millionaire or a billionaire for crying out loud, then you're going to act like that. It's the power of manifestation. It's the power of visualization. So do not get in your head.

If anything, if you're going to get in your head, you need to know what it is that you're going to do. You need to identify yourself as the outlier because you're the greatest. And you're the highest form of creation on the face of this planet. Act like it!

Honestly, you need to act like the outlier, the human being, the .1 percent that you indeed are on the face of this earth. Don't just walk around living life and carelessly not caring about your health, or your fitness, or what it is that you do.

Don't settle because when you settle, that's when you lose. That's when you become defeated. And when you grow old, that's when you have regrets. Never settle.

Being an outlier means having a lot of self-love for yourself. Some of the greatest of greats will tell you this. Self-love is one of the most powerful things as a human being that anybody can experience. And there's a lot of experiences that you can have. But self-love is by far the most important.

I'm a firm believer that every single day, it doesn't matter who you are; we can always improve our self-love. It doesn't matter how far you make it. Even the greatest of greats are still growing themselves every single day. Just because you're an outlier doesn't mean that you need to stop.

Just because you founded a multimillion or billion-dollar company, doesn't mean that you need to stop. You need to keep investing in yourself every single day. Now there are different forms of investing in yourself.

Again, as I covered in the last chapter, there are courses, books, you name it that you can invest in yourself. But if you genuinely know your difference, if you truly identify yourself as a person you know that you have different qualities, and you're unique, and you're gifted, then go out and show it.

Don't be scared. Don't be fearful. Don't fear that you're not going to impress somebody. Who cares what somebody thinks? Who cares about opinions? I had that early on. I had people say that "Nate, you're never going to be successful within the motivation or the inspiration side of things."

But here I am years later; those same people are hitting me up asking me to hang out, asking me about life, checking in on me because they know that the tables have turned.

And I know deep down inside that they wish it was different and that they were wrong. But there's that famous saying, "Kill your haters with success and just smile at them." It works.

Identify your outlier traits and use them to your advantage so you can go all in. If you need guidance and somebody to help you identify your strengths or your natural talents, or your gifts, again find a mentor.

Find somebody that'll genuinely guide you and help you get to that next level. Challenge yourself. And my challenge for you is I want you to identify your traits on what makes you who you are, what makes you the outlier, what makes you different from somebody else.

But if you want to go a step deeper, for example, if you're in business or if you're in some industry and you have somebody else that has the same position or has the same role, what makes you different from that person? What makes Steve Jobs different from Bill Gates?

You have Microsoft; you have Apple. What makes each other different from the other one? They're different products. They're different brands. But we're still human beings at the end of the day. We're still the same breed. What makes one different from the other one? And I don't want you to compete with that person. I want you to truly identify who you are and focus all in on you.

Because when you focus on you and there's that famous photo of Michael Phelps whenever he's swimming to victory in the pool. And the other guy whenever they have their arms in the air and go down in the water, up down, up down to the finish line. The other guy lifted his head and looked directly to the side at Michael Phelps.

But Michael Phelps had his vision to the end and the finish line. That's the difference in what it'll take for you to become the outlier within your entire industry and your field. Let alone the whole country and the entire universe.

Truly identify the mission that you're on, and that's just between you and yourself. You and the outlier that you're meant to be. So again, I challenge yourself to write down traits.

And as soon as you write down those traits, I want you to execute on those things. Execute on those ideas. Look online on ways that you can genuinely accomplish these things. What are some jobs that you can go after?

What are some opportunities that are good for you as a person? And genuinely go all in because you're unique. You're an outlier. You identified this. Even if you haven't recognized this yet, it's never too late. It's never early, and it's never too late to identify this. Age is just a number.

As soon as you identify yourself as an outlier, move on to the next chapter.

CHAPTER 5
"FAITH IT"

When you hear the phrase "faith it," what is it that immediately comes to mind? Is it something revolving around a religion? Is it your faith? I want you to think about you growing up. I want you to think about the moments that you had, especially as a young child, just growing up and faithing it.

I remember whenever I was a young child, growing up, going through school and, of course, being around the family, I always asked, "Hey, can I have this toy? Can I have this? Can I have that?" I always wanted things, because I knew, and I had in my mind that I'm going to get this, "I'm going to get this if I ask."

Of course, the older that we get, I feel as if the whole faithing it diminishes, because people start to say no. People begin to say, "You're not going to be able to achieve this. You're not going to be able to grow in this area. It's impossible. Whatever it is that you want to do, you're not going to do it."

We are told this lie, that we can no longer faith it anymore and that it's just not possible and it's not real. But it's something that I always wanted to do and that I always have done is that I stayed consistent with learning how to faith it.

Now, is it tough? Yes, it can be difficult, because growing up isn't easy. That's why it's called grow. You're not downing up. You're growing up. You're growing into the man, into the woman that you're meant to be. But there's little roadblocks and obstacles along the way that come in, with people not wanting you and saying no to what it is that you want to do. That's it.

That's the test. That's the test for you to say, "Okay, just because somebody tells me no, just because this happens, this circumstance came into play" ... Just because whatever it is that happened to you, you look at that, and you continue to stay consistent with your faith. You say, "It's going to work out in my favor."

I'm a firm believer that everything happens for a reason in this universe. The moment that you wake up compared to the moment that you lay your head down and go to sleep, I'm a firm believer that everything happens exactly the way that it should. The way that you eat, the people that you meet, the people that you have in your life, the way that you respond, everything is happening for a reason.

A lot of people, they feel as if everything happens just against them, but they don't look at it as it's happening as it should, every single second.

A lot of us, we've lost loved ones, and they look at that as, "Why me? Why did this happen to me?" But you need to look at it as it happened for a reason. "How can I grow from this? How can I grow from this situation?" You've got to look at the positive side always. You have to trust the process. You have to believe that everything is going exactly the way that it should, because the moment that you have doubts within what it is that you're doing, and, of course, if you doubt the plan or the process, then you're just going to diminish yourself. You're going to reduce your results. You're going to decrease the growth that you deserve.

That's one of the biggest challenges that make the average stay average compared to the successful people that keep growing, is because of the average mentality. They might trust the process, but they only believe it for so long. They can't trust it for an entire lifetime. There's going to be times where you get tested, but you have to believe it.

If you're in sales or if you're a businessman, not everybody is going to say yes to your pitch, to your product, or your service. You have to get used to that. You have to know that it's happening exactly the way that it should. With people saying no and people just telling you to leave or to get out... they don't want to buy from you, don't get offended from that. Just trust it. Trust that it happened the way that it should have.

Maybe you had this astonishing interview for this corporate job that you want, but they didn't call you back. You called them back, and they said that they'd hired somebody else. Hey, I've been there. But you know what? I trusted the process. I said, "I wasn't meant to have this job" or "I wasn't meant to land this deal" or "I wasn't meant to land this client," and then, shortly after, something better came into place.

Why? Because everything happens for a reason. I trusted the process, and, by trusting the process, I was granted an even bigger deal. I was given way better opportunities. Some of you guys need to let go of what you're comfortable with, and you need to faith it. You need to let go literally. Go after that interview. Go after that job. Go after that opportunity. Start that business. Faith it because if you're not going to faith it, you're going to regret it.

That's the name of the game. You don't want to have regret. I would ten times out of ten always take that opportunity and always go all in. Do I know that I'm going to make it out like the way that I want to? Of course not. Nobody knows that. That's why you've just got to trust yourself. Trust your gut, your instinct, and the process.

You always want to have a positive outlook on everything that you do, always say, "I'm going to do this. I'm going to hit my goals."

Think about the positive in everything, because when you do that, you have so much more potential to do what it is that you say you're going to do. If you want to write a book, say you're going to write a book, and do it. When you put that in your mind, it's more than likely going to happen.

Just because somebody gives you a not so good of a compliment or somebody might respond to you differently, don't look at it negatively. Look at it as, "Okay, they're going through something with themselves right now." Whatever it is that they're going through, I still love them for who they are. I still want to look out for them. I still have that positive outlook in them.

It doesn't matter who it is. It doesn't matter if somebody comes up to you saying how bad your shoes look or that you look funny or sound funny. Always have that positivity in you. Radiate that light, show people the way, and lead by example.

Show them that there is light. Get up to the podium on the stage. Give that speech. Tell them that it is possible to go after what you want, that it is possible to go out and make your dreams become a reality because you said it is. Most people need a voice. They need somebody to give them authority, and a lot of people, they don't have that person to provide them with authority, because they don't know where to find them.

But if you can go up there with passion, with confidence, just being you, and faithing it, you're going to shed so much light on so many people. You look at these big-time speakers, these big-time athletes, entrepreneurs, and you look at the people that look up to them. Why do they look up to them? Because they had a mission and they had a goal, and they went all in on that.

Did they doubt the way? They might have, but they still faithed it. You don't have to be too young or too old; you can do whatever it is that you want to do, and that's why these people look up to these people, these celebrities.

What is a celebrity? When you think of a celebrity or an authority figure, it's somebody that might be making a lot of money. They might be extremely talented. Or some of them might not even be talented at all. Professional Athletes had one thing in mind, and they kept going. They kept going after that goal. They kept going after that mission, after that objective, and they got to where they want to be.

I guarantee you, they might have it all, but they truly don't think they have it all, because they're still striving for greatness. They're still striving to become great. That's one thing, as human beings, we always want to strive to be better. It doesn't matter where we're at.

But it just goes to show, somebody like LeBron James, people look up to him. People look up to his talents and what it is that he's done, and he's a role model to so many, especially to the millennial generation. He led by example. He knew what he had to do, and he went and seized what was his. That's by being one of the greatest basketball players of all time. That doesn't just happen overnight. It's endless hours, every single day, of work that you have to put in.

LeBron said, "You know what? I don't have to go to college to be great. I might go to the NBA right out of high school," he put in the reps. He put in the time. He faithed it, and the universe granted what was his.

I want you to take some time, and I want you to think, what areas in your life are you lacking faith? Is it your finances, career, or maybe relationships? How can you improve in those areas? How do you want to grow, and why do you want to improve in those areas?

Because it's one thing to have a goal, it's one thing to be one of the best or the best in your industry. But why do you want to do that? What is the reason behind that? Because if you don't have a purpose, I'll tell you right now, having faith in what it is that you want to do, it's going to be a lot more complicated than what you realize.

Write down, "What are the areas that I need to improve in? What are the strengths, which we covered earlier, that I can fill to faith it? How can I lead by example to my family, peers, friends, and business partners, that this is what we all want and what I want? How can I get them to the point where they will do the same thing that I do because of my faith and the vision that I have in me?"

Because ladies and gentlemen, let me tell you something. There's no more excellent feeling when you have a leader that is absolutely at the front of everything, and they know what they want, and they have a support system with a team behind them to back them up.

LeBron James couldn't win the NBA finals by himself. That's unrealistic. 1V5? There's no way. He has a team, but he's the one that leads the team. He's the one that's the captain. I'm not saying that the other people don't have faith, but LeBron has the most faith that anything is possible and he can conquer anything. He instills that within every single one of his teammates.

Look at some of his videos of the post-game and the pre-game pep talks, the warmups that he has with his teammates, to show you how much faith he has in them, the confidence. Maybe you need to give some confidence to your business partner or your spouse. When was the last time that you had that real conversation with them?

These are the questions that you need to ask yourself because if you want to make it to the next level and if you're going to grow your life and your business, you need to understand and, most important, you need to execute on these things.

So, again, what does faith mean to you, after you read this, how exactly are you going to apply the faith it chapter, and the faith it principle to become a better human being and to accomplish and complete what it is that you want to do?

CHAPTER 6
EXPERIENCE THE WORLD

One thing that I'm incredibly grateful and blessed for a while growing up was the opportunity to travel as much as I did for being such a young cub, a young child. I remember when I was in elementary school, middle school, and just going throughout the whole school system. Every year, my family, they always used to plan vacations for us, whether it was going to Disney World, the beach, Universal Studios down in Florida, and Mexico. All of these different trips we wanted to plan like the typical middle-class family goes on one vacation a year.

I always remember I had so much fun. I was so happy whenever I did go on those vacations because I felt like I was outside of the normal lifestyle that I used to live. Of course, being a child, I didn't overthink it because I was always in that mode, but the older that I got, in the early teens and the mid-teens, I realized, "Wow, it's great to travel. I loved it." It was just like an escape from reality. It was just truly incredible to go to different areas and experience different cultures at such a young age.

I'll be forever grateful for that, with my family being able to plan those trips, because I do realize that it's not always fathomable for every family to do. I'm from a small town, once again, where some people have never been out of this town. They've never been out of Pennsylvania. It's insane, and it just blows my mind because I can't believe it, there are so many amazing things to see. There are so many locations, cities, and places in different states and countries that one can visit, but with me being from the town that I'm from, people want to stay stagnant. They don't always want to travel, or it's not that they don't ever want to travel, they don't have the money to travel.

They have never really thought about flying on an airplane, or they may be too scared to fly on a plane. I know people back from home here where they're afraid. They're scared to not just fly on an airplane, but they're scared to go out and do new things. That's what holds a lot of people back as well. Family vacations have been so important to me early on, and I feel as if I wouldn't have traveled as much early on, I might not have wanted to travel as much later.

Another big part of the whole process with traveling is I realized that there's more to life than just staying stagnant and just staying in the same area. There's nothing wrong with not wanting to travel or to stay in the same location year after year. Again, I know people that haven't, and they're 80 years old right now. They haven't traveled outside of their city, and they're 80 years old. It's insane. It blows my mind because I'm 22 years old, and I've been to amazing places throughout the world. I've been to Europe in Sweden as well as Germany. Even Asia over in China!

I've been to Canada multiple times. I've been to Mexico. Of course, throughout the different states here in the United States, California, Florida, Texas, all of these different states. I look back because I'm 22 years old, and I'm just astonished by the places that I've been able to see. I've been, and I've seen more places than what my parents have ever seen. I think about this, and I'm just so grateful for the opportunity to do so, especially with my job and of course the business that I run, that I'm able to travel from city to city, from country to country, and continent to continent.

It's a privilege to travel and just realizing that there's more out there, but I wasn't always like this. I honestly had a closed mind. I was scared to travel, and of course, whenever you start your own business, I realized that that was part of the job and that I had to get used to it. It just wasn't something that I was always fond of doing, but then I adapted it. I got used to it, and I did it more and more again. It's just an incredible experience, just literally seeing all the different cultures, all the various mountain ranges, the deserts, the coldness, the heat, the humidity of Miami.

The Denver Rockies, the beaches in Mexico, the bitter cold in Stockholm, Sweden, having layovers in

Moscow, Russia, the Great Wall of China, the villages of Germany are incredible. There's a world out there that we all need to experience, but the only thing that's going to hold you back, maybe it's finances, but most importantly, it's yourself. You can change your outcome of what you want to do with your life and where you want to travel. Something I've done early on was traveling with my family. I always used to travel with people, even with friends.

That's all that I've known, and I thought that was honestly the only way to go was to travel with somebody, because you had fun. You're always with that person or that group of people that you travel with. You get so immune to it. You're so adapted. When the time came when I had to travel alone, I was a bit nervous. I got a little bit jittery whenever my business partner said, "Nate, you can go up to Seattle, and I'm going to shoot over to China." I hesitated a bit because I've never traveled alone in my entire life. I never really did, and I got scared. I got nervous because I didn't know what to expect.

I was always used to having somebody with me that called the shots, that did the majority of the talking. Again, I'm naturally introverted, so look at somebody as an introvert traveling alone that don't necessarily talk much, and you're put in circumstances where you do have to come out of your shell. Here's the thing though. You go from that cub to the lion. You still have moments where in your life, you're a cub.

You have areas in your life where you're still a cub, and you need to become that lion.

I still had areas where whenever I traveled, I felt uncomfortable asking somebody what the flight status is, what kind of drink that I want, what security that I should go to because when you travel alone, and you go to a completely different airport it's new to you. I remember when I landed in Seattle, Washington. I had no idea where to go to the security gate to pick up my suitcase at the baggage claim. I had no idea where to go, and I got nervous. This was just within the year. I got worried because I was like, "I have to ask somebody," but you know what? I got uncomfortable, and I asked somebody.

I said, "Excuse me, sir, or excuse me ma'am, one or the other, where about do I go to pick up my luggage?" She pointed me in the right direction, and I got uncomfortable traveling alone. Sometimes in life, you have to get uncomfortable. Growth isn't comfortable as everybody wants growth, as well as everybody, wants success. Everybody wants everything, but not everybody is willing to grow. There's a difference between that. I realized with the business that I run that I had to travel alone. I had to get uncomfortable. I look at myself now where I'm at. Of course, everything is still a work in progress, but I'm way more confident and comfortable traveling by myself now compared to where I was a year ago because it was consistent.

Consistency was key. Traveling alone has been huge in my life. You experience so much more compared to whenever you travel with somebody else. You're more tempted to go out and do things of course on your own because you're alone, but you're more tempted to try new things because you're alone. You'd be surprised by the areas and the people that you go out and meet being by yourself. You would be surprised because when you're with somebody else, you know they or that group of people can take up a decent amount of time where you don't have enough time for yourself. You can only be in the house for so long a day.

If you're extremely introverted like I am, you can only be in that house for so long until you're going to need to go out and get some food and do these things. You're going to get uncomfortable by doing that. There's going to be times where you're going to have to walk into a restaurant by yourself, trust me, fast food; it can only last for so long until it starts getting to you. Health is wealth. There's going to be times where you got to walk into restaurants all by yourself, and the host or hostess is there, especially when there's a group of women that work there waiting for people to come in, and you're the only one that walks in.

"Table for? Are you waiting for somebody?" Oh, no, there's just one of me. "Okay." You got to get used to that. You have to get used to going into the grocery store, going grocery shopping by yourself. These are the little things that people don't quite understand. Whenever you travel, they look at all the places that you go to, but they don't look at these little tasks and these other things that you have to do. That's honestly one of the main steps into really just surviving while traveling. If you're traveling alone, it's massive.

Whenever you travel, you become free. For example, let's look at an airplane. When you're in an airplane, no one can access you besides the people on that plane unless you have the Wi-Fi or something, but typically, most of the time, it's just you in the air, 35,000 or 30,000 elevations up. I forget the number, but it's just you in the air. You're the only one up there as nobody can reach you. It's just you. You're free. You can become more in tune with yourself. Same with traveling, you can become free of the typical environment that you're around.

Again, I'm from a small town, not a lot of hype going on around here. You got farmlands, the Amish horse and buggies riding around here. When I go to a bigger city, again, it gets me uncomfortable, but I become free. I say, "Wow, this is completely different." I become that free version, and I love it.

The next thing I wanted to go over is some travel hacks. I just wanted to drop some value in this part of the book. Some travel hacks, something I'd recommend, and there's going to be a few here, I recommend first, a rewards program.

If somebody is looking to travel and start flying, even if it's just taking the train or taking a bus, a Greyhound bus, for example, you need to enroll in their rewards programs. I'm not saying the programs where you have to get a credit card or anything like that. Each airline (United, Delta, American, Jet Blue, Alaska, Spirit, etc.) or train as we have one train here in the U.S. Amtrak's a big one. Each bus line, Greyhound, is a big one here. They each have their own rewards programs, so you sign up for that. When you sign up, you become a member for free. Since you're a member, each flight that you book through that particular airline and once you enter your code, your flight number, and once you take that flight and land in your destination, that counts as flight miles.

Each airline calls them different rewards. I'm particularly with United Airlines, so those count as mileage plus rewards which add up. Whenever you add the numbers up, each flight that you take, they accumulate. For example, I currently have 25,000 United Airlines miles. With 25,000 United Airlines miles, that's good for about two flights depending on where the flights are, of course. I should say that's good for two trips from the east coast to the west coast here in the United States. That's just by accumulating rewards on previous flights.

Same goes whenever you eat on the flight, if you order food, it'll count for that as well. It accumulates, which is great. I highly recommend getting a rewards program. Same if there's a train, do the same thing with Amtrak. Same with the Greyhound bus as you can gain points, which helps over time. I will cover a little bit of the credit card thing as well. I'm not a credit professional. I just have been educated in a decent amount of areas, and I know loopholes that a lot of people don't quite know.

I know there's plenty more out there, but I just wanted to go over a couple of quick ones with you. Something else that's great for traveling is having your own airline's credit card. Here in the United States, there's American Airlines, United Airlines, Alaska Airlines, Southwest Airlines, Delta Airlines and all of these different airlines that you can fly. I have the United Airlines credit card. You can go on various sites to look at where the best credit cards are. A good website I recommended is uscreditcardguide.com

This site will go over a list of the current credit cards and the ongoing rewards that they have because they all change every month or every couple of few months depending on the card. I recommend getting a credit card. I recommend getting a travel card. Again, I'm with United. I have the United mileage plus credit card. With that, every time I fly with United, I don't have to pay for a checked bag. There are two United cards. I have the basic one. With the basic one, I don't have to get a checked bag, or whenever I check a bag, it's for free.

Every time I use that credit card, I accumulate miles. If I spend $10 at a restaurant, that counts as 10 miles for that credit card. It accumulates into miles because I'm getting rewarded since I have that credit card. I used to think that just having a debit card was the way to go. I thought that having a credit card was terrible. I didn't think it was good. Then I realized, "Well, I'm not in debt, so it's not like that matters. I never went to school. I don't have student loans or anything like that."

That's when I decided to get my first card, and then I realized since I travel all the time, I need to get an airline card that I always travel on. I got United. Just the perks that you can get are incredible. There's a bunch of other credit cards out there as well that I have to take advantage of the perks, but again, guys, rewards programs are crucial when you're traveling. You don't want to travel and not get rewarded for it. Every time you travel, you should be accumulating points. Same with restaurants, going out to eat, there are apps out there that you can use to collect reward points.

Starbucks, they have an app you can use to get free drinks. There are coupon codes that you can use for Chick-Fil-A, that's another one, they give you free treats. Take advantage of these offers. Whenever you travel, don't just travel and pay for everything. There are little loopholes around this, but you have to research. Rewards programs are huge. In terms of flights, I get asked this a lot about what are the cheapest flights? What's the best site that you can go on to book flights? One that I typically always use is Skiplagged. Another one that I've heard of that's pretty good is called Hopper.

The reason I use Skiplagged is it by far has the cheapest flights out there. I've never seen anything cheaper than them, to be honest with you. They're not too well known, but they're good because for example, if somebody doesn't need to check their bag and they take a carry on, the way Skiplagged works is let's say you're traveling from Chicago down to Miami. If you're flying from Chicago to Miami, but your actual layover aka your real destination is Houston, Texas.

Your main goal is to go to Houston, Texas. That's where you want to go, but this flight goes to Miami. What Skiplagged does is since you don't have a checked bag, you're still going to take that flight that goes from Chicago to Miami, but when you have that layover in Houston, you're just going to get off at that layover. Of course, you could be flying to Miami, but you're not because you got off. That's the way that Skiplagged works if you don't have a checked bag.

Even if you do have a checked bag, it's still typically a lot cheaper anyways. I believe Hopper does the same thing. Something else that's crucial, I just got it the past year, TSA Pre and Global Entry.

TSA is one of the quickest ways to get through security. There's now a faster way called Clear where it just scans your eyes or fingerprint. I know in some airports, they're changing that, but TSA Pre has always been known as the quickest way. You don't have to take your shoes off. You don't have to take much of anything off. You still do have to take your laptop out of the bag in some airports, but it's really quick. For example, if your flight is within the hour, you don't have to stress about the regular security lines. You can get through within five minutes depending upon the airport.

I'd say the quickest TSA Pre line I got through was one to two minutes, super fast, absolutely a game changer. I believe it's $100 a year. That also includes Global Entry as well. Global Entry is whenever you fly to a different country, for example, if you fly to Canada, you got to enter into customs and answer all those questions. Then they have a regular line you can go through as they're the people that don't have Global Entry.

Then there's the Global Entry that you can go through where it's instant. It's express and a priority just like an amusement park. They have that fast express, and then there's a standard line. You're that fast express and the priority. It's funny; you get looks from the other people as well that see you going through quick. The crazy part is a lot of people are just merely uneducated on TSA Pre. A lot of people tend to think the TSA Pre is only strictly for business. They think it's a huge expense, but whenever I finally did the research, which was when I got into the credit card game, I realized that it's not that bad.

It's an incredible investment if you travel a lot. It's $100, which is not that bad at all to invest, and that lasts I believe for five years. There's a credit card that you can get with Chase bank. It's one of the top cards. It is called the Chase Sapphire Reserve. That comes with Free TSA Pre as well as Global Entry, so you don't have to pay, which is fantastic. That's just one of the great perks that card comes with. Something else to include with TSA and Global Entry, you do have to get an interview for that.

Myself, I had to go to Washington, DC, as that was the closest area to me, and Washington, DC has enormous security. It took me about an hour to get everything done with, but the interview lasted about 15 minutes. They were asking me general questions, verifying my identity, and then they'll give you your ID card in the mail. You'll get express shipping a Global Entry and a TSA Pre card. They'll have you put it in this protective case. That way, people can't scan it to hack your identity whenever you're traveling.

Airbnb, I use that a lot whenever I travel. In my opinion, they're a lot cheaper than hotels. You can find incredible Airbnb's. They're people's homes that they rent out or their own space that they'll rent out half the house or an entire apartment. If you have the budget and if you want to host parties, events, or do some conferences, networking events, you can rent out an entire mansion. They are a little bit pricier if you do that, but worth it, especially if you get a group of buddies to go all in on it.

If you're on a budget, you can also find Airbnb's that run 20 bucks a night. I remember one Airbnb my business partner, and I stayed at as it was an actual camper, a motor home in Washington, DC. We did it just for the experience as it was incredible. You can stay on people's houseboats that are on the water. You can stay in people's tents. I've had one bad experience with one, but other than that, it's been great.

In my opinion, they're a lot cheaper than hotels because if I stay in hotels, they're typically the higher end ones, like the Trump, Hilton, or the Marriott. I have a Marriott credit card as well where I get points off that. There are also some personal travel hacks that you can do to have more efficient energy as I'll go over some with you. I recommend investing in some blue blocker glasses. I know Swannies are pretty well known, or, again, if you're on a budget, you can go on Amazon. Look up blue blocker glasses, and see which ones would work best for you.

I have this one pair that costs $25. They're gaming glasses, but they're blue blocker glasses, which eliminate all blue light because late at night, for example, if we have the TV on or if we're on our phones, that light can impact our sleep. That causes our circadian rhythm to be thrown into whack for hours at a time, so we might not sleep the deepest compared to if we didn't have a TV on or if we weren't on the phone a lot more compared to what we are. You slip these bad boys on, these blue blocker glasses and they'll eliminate the blue rays as much as they can, and you don't want to take them off until all of your lights are off at night.

As soon as you turn the lights off at night, and you're ready to go to bed, take them off. Put them in the case or just lay them out, and then you'll sleep like a baby. For more information on the blue blocker glasses, I do recommend you check out Shawn Stevenson's book called, "Sleep Smarter." He's the guru when it comes to that as well as another book I recommend, and I'll be going over this for the next one, is called, "Headstrong," by Dave Asprey. Those two are absolute gurus when it comes to sleeping better and just becoming and staying in that peak performance of yourself.

When traveling, whenever you're in an airplane, those lights that are in the aircraft, they're very harmful to not just your eyes but your skin, so whenever you get off an airplane, at least myself, my eyes always used to burn. They always burned every time I got off. I always felt groggy and tired. Then I realized by reading Dave Asprey's Headstrong book, that when putting those glasses on in the plane, it eliminates that, because airplane air is the worst air for you to breathe in, but if you have those blue blocker glasses on, it helps eliminate that extra light from those airplanes.

They're very harmful light rays that are getting exposed to you and your skin. It's also very crucial to not layer up but to cover as much skin as you can. If you like to wear hats, good news for you, wear hats on planes, because that light can come down and hit the top of your head, the skull region, which can also cause you to decrease in energy levels a decent amount, so try to cover as much of your skin. Wear long sleeves. This is all from the book Sleep Smarter as well as Headstrong.

It's funny; Dave was talking about whenever he goes into planes, he has people that look at him because he's wearing those glasses. He's wearing a hat. He's wearing all these different weird clothes, and people look at him funny. I actually had this experience. I don't wear hats as I'm not a big hat person myself personally, but I had those glasses on, and whenever

I went through the airports, everybody was looking at me. I felt like a celebrity, but I recommend that. Again, you want to cover the skin as well.

Another thing to do while traveling is to sanitize. I watched a video on Facebook about two months ago where they did germ tests and a sanitization test on the different things while traveling. For example, if it scores more than a 300, it's marked as you have a high risk of getting sick. They did the inside of whenever you go through security, and you put your belongings in that tin for them to run through the scanner. They mark that as having one of the highest scores in germs. I believe that it rang 2,500 out of 300. That is the absolute dirtiest on the germ scale.

Keep that in mind, whenever you do go through the security checkpoint, try not to scatter everything through that. What I like to do because you can't avoid them, and again, I have TSA Pre, so I typically don't have to use the whole one. I usually use the smaller ones, but I recommend stacking everything. If you have a wallet that you have to put in there and your computer, I recommend putting it all in one pile instead of scattering it throughout the bin, because if you spread it, the more germs will get on that. I'm a big germaphobe as well, so I try to watch all of this.

The seatbelt is another dirty one. Try not to touch that as much, and of course the tray table, that's the second highest in germs. I believe that scored a 1600 or 1700, which was insane! I do recommend if you love using that tray table, and if you're not trying to get sick, go cop yourself some baby wipes. Get yourself some hand wipes from the airport or bring them with you.

Just because you've got baby wipes doesn't mean that they're just for your child. You can also use them to sanitize the seatbelt buckle or the tray table and all these different things. I mean, even if you want to disinfect the air vent up top, you can do that. It's very crucial to your health. Another example is in a hotel, one of the dirtiest things is the television remote. If you do stay in Hotels or even Airbnb, I do recommend sanitizing that remote because people don't think to sanitize that.

Those are just some of the travel hacks. To end this chapter right here is I challenge every single one of you if you don't have one already is to create a rewards account with these airline companies. I recommend creating a rewards account with every single airline.

If we're talking overseas to go to Canada, Air Canada is one. United Emirates, Dublin, I think that might be one. Again, you get the point. I recommend creating rewards for every single one of those because you can stack it up every single time, especially going overseas, with all the miles that you accumulate with that particular airline. I challenge you to create a rewards account with the airline companies as well as the train line and if they have that in bus lines as well.

I also challenge you to book a trip. I'm from a small town that people typically don't go out. If you're reading this and you're from a small town, I want you to book a trip. Even if you got to travel one hour away, at least one hour, I challenge you. If you don't want to make a big trip to another city or you don't have the biggest of budgets, travel one day to a hotel or motel. Don't just stay in the hotel. You can if you want to, but go out a little bit. Go out and experience nature. Just walk around. Get to know yourself. Become more in tune with yourself.

You have to get uncomfortable, and that's crucial. Trust me. Do this. Do this. Do this. Do this. If you're from a bigger city, I challenge you, and maybe you do have a budget or vice versa, if you're from a smaller town and you do have a budget, I challenge you to book a trip outside of the state, even if it's just a state over.

If you want to go a little bit more extreme, go to the entirely different side of the country. Go down south. Go up north more. If you want to take it to the furthest extreme, and you have a big budget, travel overseas. You're going to learn so much more. One of the hardest things for me was traveling to Germany and not knowing how to speak German. I did not know what to say, and I was even with somebody. If I was by myself, you can imagine how that would have been, but you're going to learn so much more just by traveling. I challenge you to create a rewards program. I also challenge you to book a trip. I want you to do this within the month.

I give you this 30-day challenge and for you to complete it within a month. As soon as you do this or as soon as you get to that hotel, the motel, or the destination, I want you to tag me on social media. I want you to tag me @natethegreat on Instagram. Just give me a shout out on Facebook and say, "Nate The Great." I want you to tag me, and I'll show you guys some love on your photos, and I'll also engage with you. I'd be more than happy to do that.

Anyways, that's my challenge for you. Get uncomfortable because when you get uncomfortable, that's where you grow, and I want you to experience the world.

CHAPTER 7
ACTIVATE YOUR INNER LION

As we come to an end in this last chapter, you can see throughout my life the different things that I've gone through. The environments that I've been around and heard about how I was raised. Now we've gotten to this point where it's all about activating your inner lion. I want to ask you, what does it mean to activate your inner lion? What is your inner lion? These are some questions that you need to take the time to think about. If you want to become that beast and dominate your lane and industry, you need to know what your inner lion is, and how to activate that.

As you can see with myself, turning into a lion, I decided that I'm going to come out of the town I'm from being the most well-known there is. And it's starting to happen. I've gotten to the point where, whenever I go to some cafes back home that people come up to me now. I remember this one girl. She came up, said she followed me on Instagram, and wanted my autograph like I'm some baseball player. I've never had that in my entire life. And that's when I realized, wow, the power of influence. The power of consistency. That's what we're going to talk about here throughout this chapter.

I've traveled over and over again. I've done all these things, and I'm just 22 years old. And I've realized the potential that I've had all of this time, and it's just added up. It's added up every single step, every single inch. Something I want you to ask yourself, ladies and gentlemen is, what's your gift? Nate, this is so overused. I hear this all the time about gifts, what's your gift, blah blah blah. But I genuinely want you to take the time to ask yourself, what is your gift? I've covered earlier what some of my biggest strengths are. I know that my gift is being able to connect with anybody in this world. I've realized that at a young age, which is why I've been able to get where I'm at today. Because I'm ready to connect with anybody and everybody, it doesn't matter if it's somebody that might be homeless on the streets, it doesn't matter if it's with some big celebrity. I can connect with everybody, and I know that because that's my gift. Of course, I'm a great listener, I know all these different attributes that are also my little presents, but my gift is being able to connect with anybody.

I want to ask you again, what is your gift? What is it that you're good at? What is that one trait, or that one ability, that you're focused on the most? Superman was able to fly. That was his most significant gift. What is it that you can do that not many people can necessarily do? Yes, people can connect, but can they connect in your way? Most likely not. There's only one of you in this world. You need to realize and understand who you are as a person. So what's your gift? What are you good at? What profession is it that you're currently in? Is that the profession that you want to be in? Is that what you're gifted at? If not, take up something else as a side hustle.

I highly recommend that. If you're working a corporate job right now, and you realize that's not what your gift is, and your gift is doing something with painting, or you think you're really good at driving cars because every time you drive home in a rush, you're over there swerving in and out of other cars and you think you have the possibility of being a NASCAR driver.. Whatever your gift is, you need to try it. You can't just say, okay, I'm just going to settle. No! That's the average mentality. Don't settle. Never settle. Always progress.

The process is absolutely everything. Everybody wants success, but not everyone is willing to get success, and to achieve success. Everybody wants growth, but not everybody deserves growth. The people at the top, they are there for a reason because they went through the process. The process is not all sunshine and rainbows. There's that famous quote that Rocky Balboa says, "The world ain't all sunshine and rainbows. It's a very mean and nasty place, and I don't care how tough you are, it'll beat you to your knees and keep you there permanently if you let it. You, me, or nobody is going to hit as hard as life, but you have to be willing to take the hits. You gotta be willing to keep moving forward." I tried to memorize that as much as I can. There are more words to that. You have to live by that quote, the famous Rocky quote. "You don't wanna point fingers and blame other people, saying it was him or her or anybody! Cowards do that, and that isn't you. You're better than that!" I highly recommend watching that movie. Rocky Balboa.

You have to identify the process truly. Life is going to hit you in your face. But what are you going to do? How are you going to react? If you get hit, are you going to stay down? Heck no, you're not going to stay down. It doesn't matter the upbringing that you had. Some of these big-time athletes and sports figures, they lived in houses with 10 to 20 people. They had to sleep on the floor; they had to sleep on the streets. They've almost gotten murdered and killed. They've gotten held at gunpoint with a gun to their head, even in their mouth, and they're a success. They made themselves a success, and they worked hard. So what if somebody's six foot nine? It doesn't matter. It doesn't mean that they're just going to make it to the NBA. They have to work to get to the NBA.

These are the things that you need to realize about the process. The process, again, it's not all sunshine and rainbows. You're going to go to hell and back. There's going to be nights where you might be in an airport with no money to your name, and you have to do several calls, to try and close a deal to make it back home. That's what I had to do. For crying out loud, we were in Stockholm, Sweden, with nothing to our name. We had a 16-hour layover in Moscow, Russia, and didn't know how to speak Russian. And they didn't even have any Wi-Fi until we had to talk to this one Russian girl who worked there. All we could do was smile, and she gave it to us. These are the things that people don't want to talk about, because they don't feel comfortable talking about it. But you need to realize that it's part of the process. You're going to get hit down, but you're going get back up. Get knocked out five times, get back up six times. End of story. Show people that you can do whatever it takes. You are the highest version of yourself. Act like it!

Another trait I want to cover is patience. Patience, patience, patience. Personally, myself, that's another one of my most significant attributes is having patience. Being patient and the process, all go hand in hand. Patience is by far, one of the greatest virtues that one can have. I've never seen so many entrepreneurs, or I should say, wantrepreneurs, that want it so bad. People want success, people want that job so bad, but they tend to spoil it by not being patient. They're very impatient. They're so persistent that it literally throws people off, and they don't want to work with them, hire them, or even associate themselves with them. Just because having impatience is very annoying. But for the people that have patience, it's enormous. Especially in relationships. I can cover that in a whole different book.

Having patience in relationships, and of course, just business partnerships is by far one of the most significant traits that you can have in a partnership/relationship. Where you both can talk it out and have that patience, and truly understand each other. Do you know the guy that founded KFC? He has a white beard and hair with glasses. He was in his 50s and 60s when KFC came to life. Do you know how much patience you need to have for that? That's a lot of patience. I'm 22 years old, and I'm thinking, man, for me to wait until 65 for that thing to truly pop? That's incredible. So, I want you to ask yourself, how is your patience? What is currently going on in your life where your patience is getting tested? Maybe it's some drama at home, or you're getting into a bit of a disagreement with your boss/colleagues at work. Perhaps you don't have the patience in yourself. You feel as if it doesn't exist. How can I develop more patience? One of the ways that you can become the best version of yourself and develop more patience is genuinely taking the time to realize who you are — taking the time to find out your true inner self. Your inner lion. Read books. That's huge. Take time for yourself every single day. Patience is everything.

The next principle is execution. This one is huge. Execution... like ET (Eric Thomas) says execution is worshiped. End of story. Execution is worshiped. Like I covered earlier in the previous chapter, you don't remember the number two or the number three guy. You always remember the number one guy and the number one team, because nobody cares about the other ones that didn't make it — the end of the story. People only want to know the people that executed and finished. So when it comes to execution, how great are you of an executor? And I want you to be honest with yourself. I don't want you to lie to yourself, because when you lie to yourself, you're living in a false reality. And it's just going to set you up for failure.

How well of an executor are you? Are you the type that, when you tell somebody that you're going to be at a destination at a specific time, are you a man of your word? Are you a woman of your word? Do you execute on that note? Do you tell people things and always come through? If so, you're an executor. How long does it take you to do a task? Do you tell people, "Listen, I'm going to have this task done by this date," is it done by that date? Is the project finished? And if it's not, you're not an executor. Little things like this are enormous. When you can truly become a full out executioner and learn how to execute, you have such a massive advantage in this world to succeed. It doesn't matter what it is that you do.

I covered patience just a little bit ago. Because some things require patience, you can't just paint a world class painting within five minutes. I mean, you can, but if you're trying to make an impact, it takes time. You have to have patience if you want to paint. If you're going to bang out that business task or get promoted. Maybe you have to sell more credit cards or sell more phones, memberships, and plans. Perhaps you're a team leader already, and you have to make sure everybody is on track to hit their goals. How are you going to execute all of this? Perhaps you need to jot down the number of actions a day you need to complete. By me doing X amount of calls, X number of walk-ins, door knocks, or hand out X number of flyers that I'm going to hit this goal by the end of the week, day, or by the end of the month.

Take the time to track your goals. Because let me tell you something, a lot of people say, "Nate, I'm an executor, but it just doesn't happen." Typically, most of the time, ten times out of 10, they don't track their goals. You might be an executor, but you're still living that false reality in your head because you don't have your goals written down. How do you expect to execute on a task to its entirety if you don't exactly know what you're aiming to hit? That's just like me having a blindfold over my eyes, and somebody saying, "Okay, Nate, hit the target. Shoot the target." I'm going to say, "Where is it at?" "Well, you have to guess." That's what you're doing with your goals because you're not writing them down. If you had your goals written down, of course, they might say, "Hey, hit the target, Nate." But this time I don't have a blindfold on. And I can look around to see where the target's at, and then hit the mark. Hit the bullseye. Again, execution is worshiped. Remember that.

Next up is consistency. Consistency, consistency, consistency. That right there... and I put this after execution because it's one thing to execute, it's another thing to be consistent. For example, on the smaller tasks... if somebody's trying to put out video content. Great! You executed on one video. Where's your next video? Where's the consistency behind these videos? Where's the consistency behind you? Just because you tell somebody you're going to do this, and you do it once, or a couple of times, that's great. But how consistent will you be? Guys, the top people in their industries, they're consistent. Every single day. They wake up at a particular time; they go to bed at a specific time. They're consistent. Gym in, gym out. They eat a certain way. It's next level. They're in that lion state. Their inner lion. They know themselves, and they're consistent with themselves. They have that balance in their lives, which is what a lot of people want.

You have to learn to be consistent with your actions. Again, execution is worshiped. That's great, but how consistent are you going to be with executing? If you can execute, first off, and you're also consistent, those two alone are going to win you big in this life. If you're super consistent and if you know how to execute, and you feel as if you still haven't made it yet or you're still having a hard time, I want you to personally reach out to me and send me a message on social media. I want to help you guys win so much if you have execution and consistency down pat that is.

You look at some of these big sports teams, and a lot of these big-time music artists. There's a reason that there are only one hit wonders, and you don't hear about them again. It's because they're not consistent. End of the story, look at the Michael Jacksons of this world. Look at the Stevie Wonders, the Justin Biebers. Look at these individuals that are dominating their industry. Drake. As far as I know, Drake's released an album every year for the past five years, maybe even more. It's because he's consistent. People ask, "I don't know if Drake should be the greatest rapper of all time." Why not? He may not be the greatest of all time, but he's up there. Why shouldn't he be in the top three, or the top five? He's way more consistent than half of these rappers.

Consistency is everything. It doesn't matter what it is that you do. If you're in business, how many calls are you going to do every single day? How many meetups do you have to do? Think about that. Same with relationships. How many hours a week do you need to dedicate or every single day, to your spouse, to make sure he or she and both of you, are on the same accord? Another great book I recommend, "The Five Love Languages." I believe that's by Gary Chapman. If your spouse's love language is quality time, you best be giving them some quality time because that's their love language. Be consistent with your actions. Be consistent with your duties, and you'll see a change in your life.

Peak performance is another one. What is it every single day that gets you in your peak performance? I like this one saying, by Kendall Ficklin, he says, "I don't wake up on 10. I wake up on zero and work my way to 10." So what does he mean by that? "I don't wake up at a 10." I don't wake up feeling incredible like I'm ready to crush the world. Of course, we're going to wake up a little bit tired. We wake up on a zero, working our way to a 10. For example, maybe it's getting that coffee in the morning or getting that workout in, like a lot of these athletes do. It's like a meditation to them, is working out. That's what gets them in their peak performance. Some people, they drink certain beverages to make them feel a certain way. They sniff some stuff. Other people, they use drugs to get them in their peak state, like marijuana, or weed. It's whatever works best for them. I do not recommend doing any harmful drugs like cigarettes or anything that doesn't positively help your state of mind.

Maybe it's a specific breathing exercise. Tony Robbins, he's excellent at this. If you go on YouTube and type in "breathing technique peak performance," one video is going to pop up on how to get in your peak performance state and that abundance mentality to start your day. It feels wonderful. Meditation is when it comes to being in your peak performance.

Let's go through a routine schedule here. Let's say you wake up at a zero. You get out of bed and have a glass of water beside you. You drink the whole glass right away. So you go from zero to one. Your body is naturally dehydrated whenever you're asleep since no fluids are coming in your system. So you drink some water, you get your shower and refreshed, so you go from one to two. And then from two, after you get your shower, you get all dressed for the day, you feel good, put on some perfume or cologne, you go from two to four because you feel more confident about yourself. You don't have the pyjamas on anymore; you're sticking your chest out a little bit and walking tall. So you go from two to four there.

From four, you go downstairs, or you go out, either or, and you get some coffee. You go to Starbucks to get your coffee, or maybe you make your coffee at home. I recommend bulletproof coffee, fantastic coffee. Perhaps for you, it could be tea or some other type of drink that gets you flowing. For some of you guys, you might go from a four to a six. Let's say the average person goes from a four to a six after that. So you're at that six. And if you're already at a ten, wow. That's incredible. There are way many more things that you can implement in your life. So, if you're at that six, and you drink that coffee or tea, maybe you need to get some breakfast. Get something into your system like some food, get some dopamine rushing into your brain, so you go from six to eight.

But you're not entirely at your peak performance yet. What else do you need to do to get to your peak performance? Maybe you need to do some meditation. Let's say you meditate a little bit, and you get in that abundance mentality, that gratefulness. You say a prayer, and you go from eight to nine, but you're still not there yet. What else needs to happen for you to get there to maximize your day truly? Maybe it's yourself going to your loved one, saying you love them before you leave to go to work or you give your kids a hug and a kiss. Maybe it's you are setting up their meals and serving them before they head off to school or hugging them goodbye before they go to school, and that maximizes you to hit your ten. Maybe your ten doesn't come until you do something very productive at work. Either way, you need to hit that peak performance every single day. Each one of our peak performances is entirely different. We might have the same habits, but we all have triggers that make us click daily.

Test it out. If you have trouble with a routine in the morning or an evening routine, test it so you can get in your inner peak performance. Same with a night mode, having your night peak performance. Again, blue blocker glasses. They're great to wind down for the night. Instead of watching TV an hour before bed, try reading a biography book an hour before bed. Turn the phone off an hour before bed. Do these little things. Get into your peak performance. You can find all of this stuff in "Sleep Smarter," as well as "Head Strong." If you want to get into your peak performance and accomplish all of your goals and tasks, you need to get into this performance mode. This beast mode. It's crucial for your success — 100%.

So on this final note. I always want you to keep in mind; we're continually growing as human beings. All the principles that I've gone over, all of the hacks and the experiences that I've been through in my life, just in this book, I want you to take it, and I want you to learn from them. Maybe you've experienced more. Great. Perhaps you haven't done as much yet with your life, and you want to do more. This is perfect. It doesn't matter what your circumstance is. What matters is you want to grow, and you being okay with growth and getting uncomfortable. That is my wish for you, just by reading this book, is for you to grow as a human being truly and for you to activate your inner lion indeed. We all have an inner lion within ourselves, but it needs to get activated. With the steps throughout these chapters I've provided you with, I truly wish you the best in your success, for you to activate your inner lion. And please, keep me updated throughout your journey. Tag me on Instagram and social media. Let me know that you're striving and you're continuing to push for greatness. I'll for sure engage and interact with you; I'll do it all. I appreciate you for reading, now be GREAT!